D0534011

Learning every secret in Minecraft takes forever! Even someone who plays every day might miss some tricks and shortcuts that could transform the way they play. That's why we've put together this list of 101 secrets, tips and tricks used by experts the world over, to turn you from a Minecraft newbie into a Minecraft pro!

Mineworld Cheats Guide - 978-1-78106-507-5

Published by Dennis Lifestyle Ltd. 30 Cleveland St, London W1T 4JD. Company registered in England no. 1138891.

DISCLAIMER

A SMARTER INVENTORY

1

Organise your inventory quickbar so that your torches, tools and weapons are within easy reach.

2

Keep lava buckets around – they're 12 times better than a piece of coal for powering a furnace.

3

Iron ingots are very useful – they appear in 27 different crafting recipes, so stock up on them!

4

You can destroy unwanted blocks by throwing them into lava, into a fire or at a cactus.

Wood is rare underground. You need it to craft many common items, so if you explore a cave make sure to take some logs with you!

5

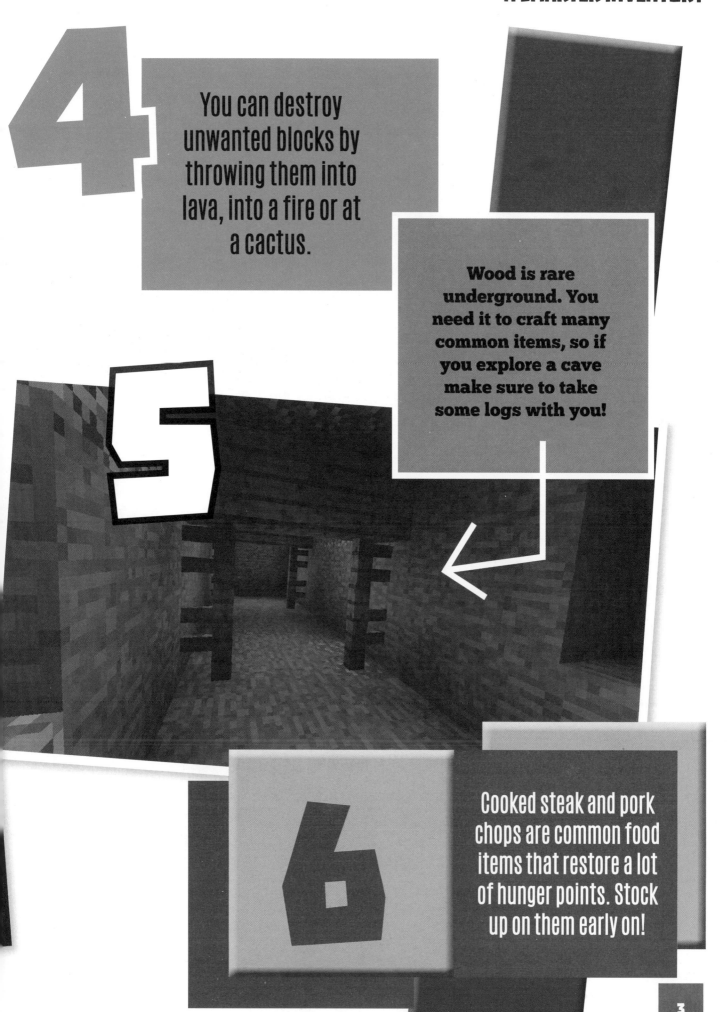

6

Cooked steak and pork chops are common food items that restore a lot of hunger points. Stock up on them early on!

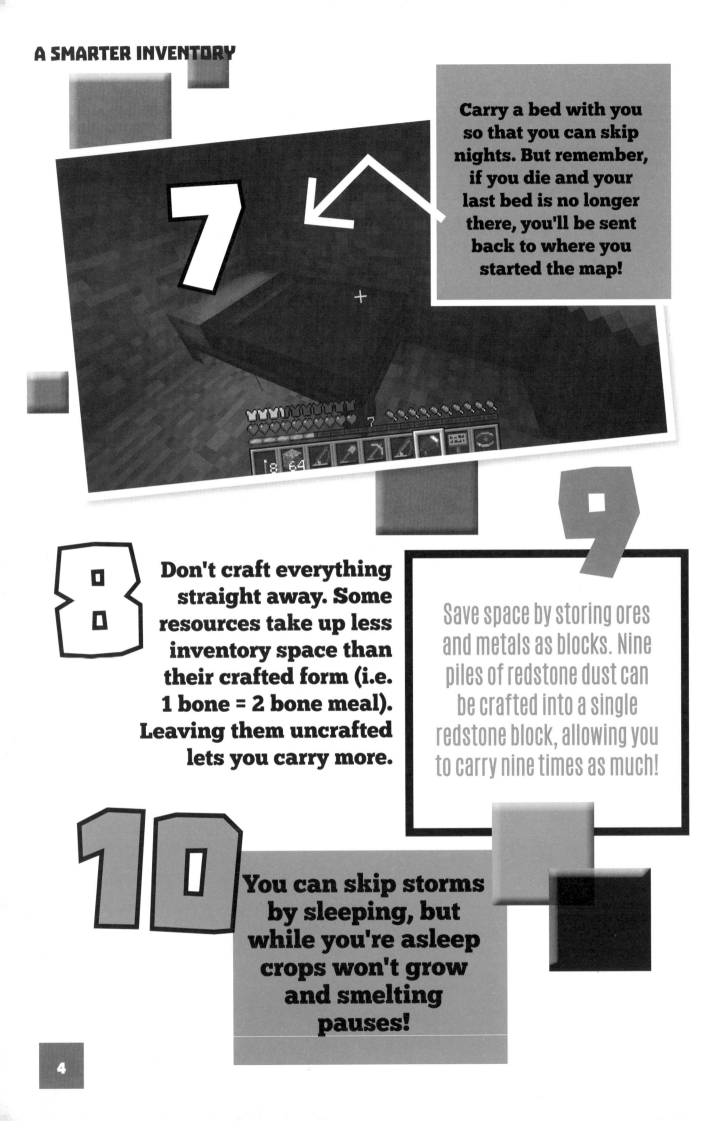

7

Carry a bed with you so that you can skip nights. But remember, if you die and your last bed is no longer there, you'll be sent back to where you started the map!

8 Don't craft everything straight away. Some resources take up less inventory space than their crafted form (i.e. 1 bone = 2 bone meal). Leaving them uncrafted lets you carry more.

9 Save space by storing ores and metals as blocks. Nine piles of redstone dust can be crafted into a single redstone block, allowing you to carry nine times as much!

10 You can skip storms by sleeping, but while you're asleep crops won't grow and smelting pauses!

11

Blocks will take five times longer to break if you're underwater, but keep your head dry and you can mine at normal speed.

MOVING AROUND

12

When underwater, you can quickly float to the surface by placing a boat in front of you and getting straight into it.

13

If you fall, aim for water – landing in water prevents you from taking damage when falling.

14

When sneaking, it's impossible to fall off cliffs, so if in doubt sneak everywhere!

15

Bunny hopping (sprinting and repeatedly jumping) is quicker than sprinting on its own.

16

Bunny hopping on ice is even faster!

17

Abandoned mineshafts are a good source of emergency wood if you're trapped underground.

18

Stand in a water flow when mining near lava. If you break the wrong block, the water will turn the lava to stone before it damages you.

19

Never dig directly down! There's no way of knowing if you're above a large drop or a lava lake.

20

Never dig directly up! Even if you can't see lava or water droplets, there could be a gang of mobs just waiting to drop on you.

21

Try not to dig underwater. It creates a suction current that's hard to swim through and might suffocate you!

22

Remember that you can sprint straight over one-block gaps without stopping.

23

Walking up stairs is faster than jumping up a slope. Craft stairs to make things easier for yourself!

SECRET USES FOR TOOLS & ITEMS

24 Jack 'o' lanterns and glowstones emit light even underwater.

26

25 Axes aren't just for chopping trees – they mine any wooden block faster than other tools.

Never spend too long underground. When you've collected some resources, turn back and put them in a safe place!

27 You can cast fishing rods onto pressure plates to set them off from a distance.

28 Put lily pads on water to creating simple bridges – you can walk on them!

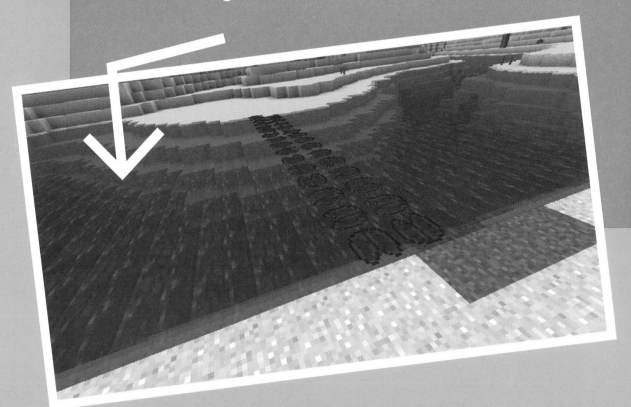

If you're making fences, remember that six Nether bricks will create six Nether brick fences, whereas six sticks will only create two wooden fences. **29**

30

To use less wood, place ladders one block apart - because the player is two blocks high, you'll still be able to climb them as normal.

31

You can use a bucket of water as a portable "elevator". Swimming up and down water flows is quicker than building a staircase!

32

If you have to fall more than eight blocks distance, teleport using an ender pearl instead and you'll take less damage.

33

Boats are much faster than swimming, so use one whenever you can!

34

When exploring underground, only place torches on the right-hand side of a cave. That way, when you want to find your way back to the surface, all you have to do is make sure the torches are on your left!

35

Half-size blocks like slabs can be used to create staircases with a more gentle incline than actual staircase blocks.

UNDERSTANDING RARE BLOCKS

36

Use a crafting table to encase a piece of redstone in wood and you'll create a musical note block.

37

Wooden slabs are fireproof. Double them up to create fireproof blocks.

38

Don't use glass blocks as windows. Six glass blocks makes 16 glass panes, so you cover more space using them!

39

You can combine lava and water to create cobblestone, stone or obsidian, depending on which of the two are flowing or still.

40

Most ore needs an iron or diamond pickaxe to be mined. Use any other type of tool, and you simply destroy the block without getting anything from it.

41

Granite, andesite and diorite look nice but aren't any stronger than normal stone.

42

You can often craft four blocks to make nicer-looking blocks: four stone creates stone bricks, and four granite creates polished granite. Try other combinations!

Prismarine can only be found in ocean monuments and takes five-and-a-half minutes to cycle through all its colours.

43

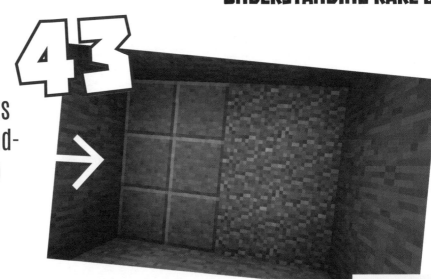

44

Obsidian is resistant to almost any form of damage, so it's great for building damage-proof shelters.

45

Sponges can absorb up to 65 blocks of water, and you can dry a wet sponge in a furnace.

46

If you fall onto slime blocks, you won't take fall damage.

47

Coarse dirt can by created by combining two gravel and two dirt, and will not grow grass.

48

You can craft mossy stone and bricks by combining vines with cobblestone or stone bricks.

49 Destroying a monster spawner gets you the most experience points in the game (other than killing a boss).

ANIMALS, FOOD & MOBS

50 Feeding sugar to horses makes them heal faster, grow quicker and tame more easily.

On a horse, you can run straight over small gaps, and jump over fences and walls.

17

52

Nether brick fences don't join up to wooden fences, so you can use a Nether brick fencepost to create a gate that lets you through but keeps animals penned in.

53

You can feed tame ocelots raw fish to get them to breed. Use clownfish, as these restore very little hunger and have no other use.

54

You can use a fishing rod to hook animals (and mobs) to lead them around.

55

Leads allow you to tie up friendly animals so they don't wander off. You can create two leads using four string and one slimeball.

56

Witches use a lot of potions. Use a bucket of milk to cure yourself once they've been killed.

57

If you want to keep a zombie or skeleton alive during the day, keep them underwater.

58

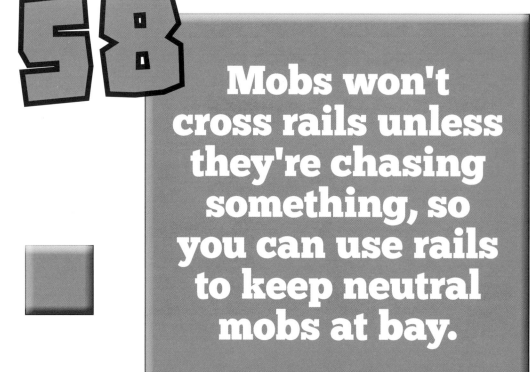

Mobs won't cross rails unless they're chasing something, so you can use rails to keep neutral mobs at bay.

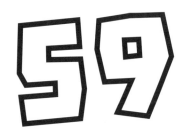

If a silverfish re-enters a block, it will be completely healed, so don't let them get away!

59

60

You can cure a zombie villager by throwing a splash potion of weakness at them then feeding them a golden apple. It takes a few minutes!

You can recognise zombie villagers from their faces - they look like green villagers, not regular zombies.

61

62

You can trap endermen by pushing them into a minecart. They can't teleport away!

COMBAT, ENCHANTMENTS & POTIONS

63

You can only find glowstone dust in the Overworld by killing witches.

64

Cauldrons can be filled with water and used to wash the dye off leather clothing, or fill three glass bottles.

65

You can combine enchanted books on an anvil to create books with multiple enchantments.

66

If you're low on weapons, remember that lava can damage most enemies. Keep a bucket handy!

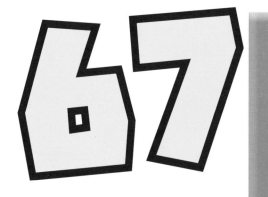

However, fire and lava have no damaging effects on mobs that spawn in the Nether.

Bows are good for killing creepers, but endermen will usually teleport away before an arrow hits them.

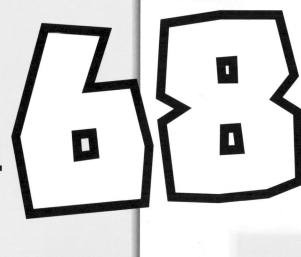

If you kill a silverfish in one hit, other silverfish won't come to its aid. Use a diamond sword when fighting them!

70

You can get lots of experience by fighting blazes. They give 10 experience points per kill, which is at least double that of most others.

71

You can heal injured villagers by trading with them or using a splash potion of healing.

72

Wither skeletons can pick up (and use) discarded bows and swords, so don't drop any nearby!

73

Baby zombies are faster and more powerful than regular zombies, so take them out first!

74

When you fight your first blaze, use a golden apple to boost your stats. After that, you can use blaze rods to make fire resistance potions!

75

If you hit an enemy while sprinting, you'll cause a greater amount of knockback. Enough to push a creeper to a safe distance!

76

You can't eat a glistering melon, but you can use it to create health-restoring potions!

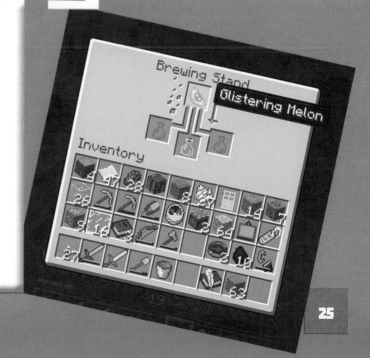

77

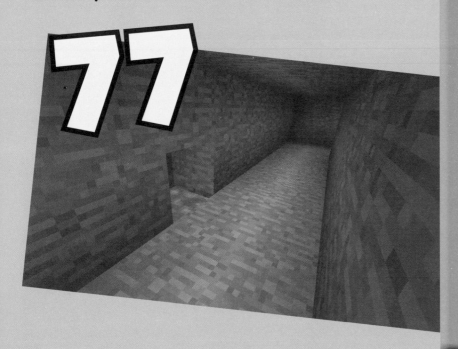

You can expand villages by building shelters with doors. Each new door increases the chance of a new villager spawning.

FUN TIPS!

78

Lava makes a great (if dangerous) light source. It's one of the few blocks that emits light level 15!

79

Maps, books and banners can quickly be copied by crafting them with a blank version.

80

You can make it easier to find jungle temples by setting jungles on fire.

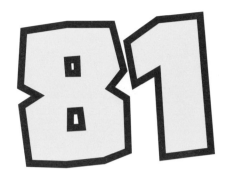

81 To play a note block, you can hit it or activate it using a redstone charge. Connect multiple note blocks with redstone to play chords!

82 The sound of a note block changes, depending on the material it's placed on.

84 Jungle temples are the only place you'll find naturally occurring pistons, levers and dispensers in the Overworld.

83 Craft dye with banners to make patterns appear. The position of the dye changes the pattern you see!

27

85

You can create an infinite water source with just two buckets of water. Dig a 2x2 pit and place one water source in each corner.

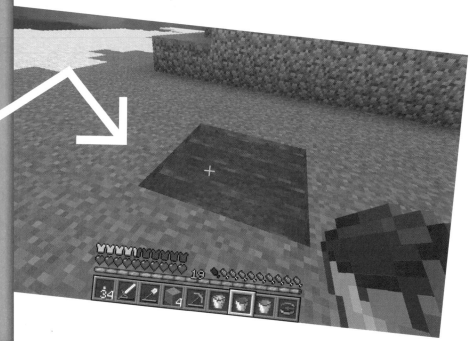

86

Minecarts travel fastest diagonally. They travel at eight blocks per second in a straight line, but 11.3 blocks a second diagonally.

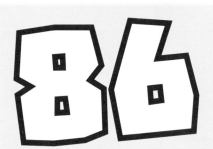

87

Riding in minecarts is 10% slower than sprinting, but you can use the time travelling to craft or reorganise your inventory.

88

Add extra lighting to villages so that mobs don't spawn inside villager's houses and kill them.

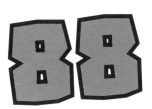

89

Snow golems can be used as an infinite source of snow. Trap them in a pen or room, and they'll leave snow wherever they walk, which you can then collect.

THE MOST ADVANCED MINECRAFT TIPS

90

Beacons can be built overlapping to save resources, as long as the beacon blocks at the top are at least a block apart.

If you build a beacon, place it near your home. This will give you the power-up effects where you need them most.

91

92

When building redstone circuits, always lay your redstone on easily identifiable blocks, such as snow or bricks. This makes sure you don't accidentally destroy them from another angle.

93

Building a portal in the Overworld will cause zombie pigmen to spawn nearby. Try to build them in a secure room or pit.

94

You can build in the End, but leave the entry platform clear. Anything built or placed on it will be erased whenever someone enters the End.

95

Some blocks behave differently in the End: plants won't grow, compasses and clocks won't work, Nether portals will fail to activate and beds will explode when placed.

96

In strongholds, you can recognise monster egg blocks because they break slightly slower than normal blocks.

97

Minecarts can travel through portals as a shortcut, but remember to protect their route from mobs!

98

Destroy the pressure plate in desert temples as soon as you find them; otherwise, a mob might spawn and set off the TNT!

99

If you repair an enchanted item on a crafting table, you'll lose the enchantment. Use an anvil instead!

100

The rarest ore in the game is emerald, but you'll only find it in the extreme hills biome. You'll need an iron or diamond pickaxe to mine it.

101

Hide in water to block the effects of explosions from TNT or exploding creepers.